A M A Z I N G
PREHISTORIC
F A C T S

Anita Ganeri
Illustrated by Andrew Laws
Consultant: Penny Wheatcroft
Series Editor: Heather Amery
Art Editor: Rowena Alsey

Contents

MALLARD PRESS

An imprint of BDD Promotional Book Company, Inc., 666 Fifth Avenue, New York, N.Y. 10103

In the Beginning

The Earth was born from a huge, spinning cloud of hot gases about 4.6 billion years ago. As the gases cooled, they formed rocks. Volcanoes covered the new planet, shooting up water vapor which formed the first, very hot seas.

At that time, the atmosphere was made up of poisonous gases, such as methane, carbon monoxide and ammonia. Lightning and fierce storms hit the Earth but the first rain quickly dried up on the hot surface.

Life Begins

At first the seas were like a chemical soup covering the Earth. The first living things grew in it about 3.2 billion years ago. Fossils of these tiny cells have been found in a kind of ancient flint rock.

A Different Map

A map of the Earth 170 million years ago would have looked quite different from a modern map. At that time, all the land was one huge continent, called Pangaea. It was surrounded by ocean. Over millions of years, Pangaea broke up into the continents we have today.

Blue-greens

Some of the first plants lived 3 billion years ago. They were tiny algae, called blue-greens. These plants have left a huge number of fossils in rocks in Africa, Australia, and in the Grand Canyon, USA.

Breathing Life

Without plants, no animals could have ever lived on Earth. In sunlight, plants give off a gas called oxygen, which all animals need to breathe. Oxygen from the plants went into the atmosphere until there was enough for animals to breathe. Today, algae still make about two thirds of all the oxygen in the Earth's atmosphere.

Did You Know?

Lightning may have caused the first life on Earth. In an experiment, scientists sent electricity through a mixture of chemicals and gases like the Earth's atmosphere millions of years ago. Amino acids, the building blocks of all living things, were formed.

About 400 million years ago, plants first began growing on land. They had no roots, leaves or flowers. About 100 million years later, forests of giant horsetails, club mosses, and ferns covered the Earth. The coal we burn now is the fossil remains of those forests.

Fossil Facts

Everything we know about early life on Earth comes from fossils. These are the prints of animals and plants which have hardened in stone over millions of years.

Protoceratops's Eggs

The chance of something becoming a fossil is very small. Usually only the hard parts of an animal, such as teeth, bones, horns and shells survive. Scientists have also found fossils of insect wings, leaves, feathers, eggs, droppings and footprints.

Ammonite

Scientists work out how old fossils are from the age of the rocks they are found in. For more accurate dates, they use a method called carbon 14 dating. All living things take in radioactive carbon atoms which decay at a steady rate. By counting how much radioactivity is left in a fossil, scientists can tell how old it is.

Life in the Sea

Fossils show that the first animals to appear in the world lived in the sea about 700 million years ago. At this time, there were no plants or animals on land.

The earliest sea creatures were jellyfish and sponges. The first shellfish lived about 570 million years ago, and the first fish about 70 million years later.

Bug Eyes

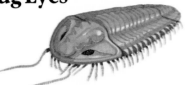

Trilobites were the first animals with complicated eyes. Each eye had up to 20,000 lenses. Some lenses are so well preserved, scientists have taken photographs with them, after 400 million years.

First Fish

The first fish had no jaws and sucked in food. Fish with jaws appeared 395 million years ago. Dinichthys, one of the fiercest, was as long as a canoe and had teeth 2 ft (60 cm) long.

Sea Facts

Ammonites were ancient shellfish which lived at the time of the dinosaurs. The biggest was wider than a car.

Pterygotus was the largest sea scorpion that has ever lived. It was as big as a crocodile and had huge pincers.

Fossils of the first known animals, giant jellyfish, were found in Australia. They died on a beach 670 million years ago.

A type of snail living deep under the sea near Costa Rica first appeared on Earth 500 million years ago. It has not changed at all since then.

In 1938 a large fish, called a coelacanth, was caught near South Africa. Scientists thought that it had died out 70 million years ago. They later found that the people on the Comoro Islands had been catching them for years.

Shark History

The ancestors of today's great white shark lived 22 million years ago. Carcharodon megalodon could open its jaws so wide that a tall man could have stood inside. Its terrible teeth were as long as a human hand.

Jellyfish

Sea Lilies

Coral

Sea Snail

Clams

Sea Reptiles

Ichthyosaurs were sea reptiles shaped like dolphins. Most reptiles lay eggs but Ichthyosaurs had live babies. We know this because scientists have found fossils of pregnant mothers.

Archelon was a giant sea turtle which lived 85 million years ago. It grew as big as a truck. This monster was quite harmless. It had weak jaws and could only eat jellyfish.

Plesiosaurs were huge reptiles which lived in the sea 210 million years ago. The longest of all was Elasmosaurus. Its neck was four times longer than a giraffe's and had 70 bones.

Did You Know?

Coral is made by tiny sea animals. Every day they build up a new band of coral. By studying these bands scientists have worked out that 400 million years ago, there were 400 days in a year. That is 35 more days than there are now.

Lakes and seas were full of plants and animals about 500 million years ago, although the land was bare and rocky. Most of the animals died out but some of the plants' descendants are still alive and have not changed over millions of years.

Crinoids

Trilobite

Sponges

Invading the Land

The first animals to live on land were fish. About 370 million years ago, a group left their homes in the swamps and struggled ashore. They developed into amphibians, the family of animals which includes frogs and toads.

Amphibians live on land but have to return to the water to lay their eggs. The first animals to live on land all the time were early reptiles. They were the ancestors of the dinosaurs.

Armor Plating

Before the dinosaurs lived on Earth, Erythrosuchus was the fiercest land animal. It was about 16 ft (5 m) long, with a huge head and sharp teeth. The animals it ate grew thick, bony plates to protect their bodies.

First on Land

The first creatures on land were called lobe-finned fish. They grew lungs to breathe air and pulled themselves out of the water on strong leg-like fins.

On Four Legs

Ichthyostega was one of the first amphibians. It had scales on its stomach and a tail, like a fish, but it walked on four legs. It lived in Greenland which was hot and damp 370 million years ago.

Hard to Swallow

One of the strangest early amphibians was Diplocaulus. Its head was shaped like a boomerang. This must have made it very difficult for its enemies to swallow it.

Reptile and Amphibian Facts

The first snakes lived about 80 million years ago. They were descended from burrowing lizards. The longest prehistoric snake was a huge python, 36 ft (11 m) long. Its ancestors are still alive.

Amphibians were the first creatures which could shoot out their tongues to catch insects.

A tortoise, Testudo atlas, was the largest tortoise ever known. It weighed as much as 60 people.

Useful Sail

Dimetrodon was a reptile with a huge sail on its back, made of bony spines covered with skin. It used its sail for air-conditioning, turning it to the sun to warm up and away from the sun when it wanted to cool down.

Did You Know?

Some of the first reptiles were only the size of small lizards. Others were huge. Megalania was three times as big as the largest living reptile, the Komodo Dragon. It lived in Australia and hunted prehistoric kangaroos.

Deinosuchus was a giant crocodile which ate dinosaurs. It grabbed them as they came to the swamp to drink. This monster weighed as much as two hippos and was three times as big as the largest crocodile today.

A relation of the prehistoric reptiles still lives in New Zealand. It is the tuatara. Now about 2 ft (60 cm) long, its ancestors were as big as sheep. Apart from growing smaller, it has not changed for 200 million years.

Giant Vegetarians

Dinosaurs lived on the Earth for about 140 million years. That is about 70 times longer than scientists think human beings have lived. They died out quite suddenly about 65 million years ago but no one really knows why.

There were many different kinds of dinosaurs. Some were fierce, with sharp teeth and ate other dinosaurs. Some lived in swamps and only ate the plants and trees. The plant-eating dinosaurs are called herbivores.

Bony Heads

Pachycephalosaurus belonged to a group of dinosaurs which were nicknamed "bone heads". Their skulls were about 10 ins (25 cm) thick and they crashed their heads together when they were fighting. No one knows if the bumps on their necks and noses were useful.

Some dinosaurs had strange shaped heads. Triceratops, which means "three-horned face", was a fierce looking herbivore. It had a big bony frill and used its three sharp horns to defend itself. Its head was about 10 ft (3 m) long.

Diplodocus

Diplodocus was one of the longest dinosaurs ever to have lived. It was about 85 ft (26 m) long and weighed about 26 tons.

As well as using its tail for balancing, Diplodocus also used it as a whip to lash out at its enemies.

Suits of Armor

To protect itself from the meat-eating dinosaurs, Nodosaurus had tough, bony plates of skin all over its head and back and tail. Its name means "lumpy lizard" and it was about 17 ft (5 m) long.

As well as a spiky suit of armor, Euoplocephalus had a very useful tail to use when attacked. The two bony lumps of skin at the end of its tail were like a huge heavy club.

It had a small head with a very small brain.

Its nostrils were on the top of its head so it could breathe with most of its head under the water.

Its neck was so long, about 25 ft (8 m), it could feed on the tops of the tall trees.

It stripped the leaves off trees but could not chew them with its weak teeth.

Its strong backbone supported the enormous weight of its snaky neck, long body and whip-like tail.

Like other plant-eating dinosaurs, Diplodocus swallowed big stones. They helped to grind up leaves and twigs in its stomach.

It walked on its four huge, strong legs, each one about twice the height of a man.

Did You Know?

Stegosaurus had a tiny brain about the size of a walnut. Its body weighed nearly 2 tons and its brain only 2 oz (55 gms).

9

Terrible Lizards

Some dinosaurs were huge creatures with massive heads and razor-sharp teeth, which walked on their hind legs. Called carnosaurs or "flesh-eating lizards", the biggest and fiercest of them all was Tyrannosaurus rex.

The other meat-eating dinosaurs are called coelurosaurs or "hollow-tailed lizards". They were much smaller and lighter than the carnosaurs and could run very fast on their hind legs. They probably ate small animals, lizards and insects.

Tyrannosaurus killed and ate other dinosaurs. It attacked with its long teeth and sharp claws.

Tyrannosaurus Rex

Tyrannosaurus rex, "king of the tyrant reptiles" weighed over 8 tons and was nearly 50 ft (15 m) long.

It used its thick tail to help it keep its balance when standing on its hind legs.

It had huge, strong legs but it probably could not run fast because it was so big and heavy.

Edmontosaurus was one of the plant-eating dinosaurs which was attacked by Tyrannosaurus. About 33 ft (10 m) long, it ate water plants, chewing them up with its duck-like jaws.

Hunting in Packs

One of the fiercest dinosaurs was Deinonychus, meaning "terrible claw". It had huge claws which it used to hold and kill its prey.

Deinonychus probably hunted in packs, sometimes attacking large plant-eating dinosaurs. They had many long, sharp teeth to bite and tear the flesh from their victims.

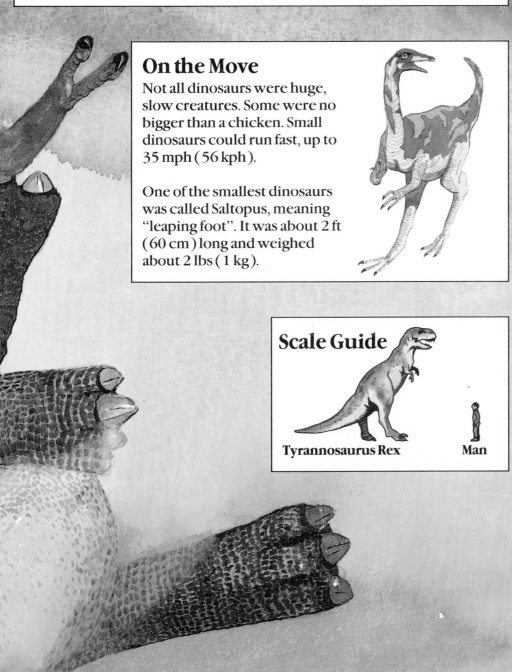

On the Move

Not all dinosaurs were huge, slow creatures. Some were no bigger than a chicken. Small dinosaurs could run fast, up to 35 mph (56 kph).

One of the smallest dinosaurs was called Saltopus, meaning "leaping foot". It was about 2 ft (60 cm) long and weighed about 2 lbs (1 kg).

Scale Guide

Tyrannosaurus Rex   **Man**

Dinosaur Facts

No one knew that dinosaurs existed until 150 years ago. When some huge bones were found in England about 300 years ago, people thought they were bones of a giant man.

In 1841, a scientist, called Dr Richard Owen, gave the dinosaurs their name. In Greek the word means "terrible lizard".

The biggest dinosaur, Brachiosaurus, is thought to have been 92 ft (28 m) long and may have weighed as much as 100 tons, about the same as 15 large elephants.

Fossilized dinosaur droppings are called coprolites. Scientists can tell from them what dinosaurs fed on.

When the fossilized bones of an Iguanodon were first found, scientists thought it had horns on its nose. Later they realised that they were not horns but a spike on each thumb.

Scientists can tell from dinosaurs' teeth what they ate. Herbivores had flat teeth for chewing up tough plants and carnivores had pointed teeth for biting and tearing meat.

Duck-billed dinosaurs, called hadrosaurs, had over 2,000 teeth in up to 60 rows. When the teeth wore out, new ones grew in their place to grind up tough water plants.

No one knows why the dinosaurs became extinct but there are many ideas. One is that they thought life was so dull, they died of boredom!

The First Fliers

Many prehistoric creatures took to the skies to avoid being eaten by hungry dinosaurs. The first animals to fly were insects, about 300 million years ago. For 100 million years, they had the air to themselves.

The insects were joined by flying reptiles, called pterosaurs. They glided on leathery wings, like giant bats. About 140 million years ago, some reptiles grew feathers and the first birds appeared on Earth.

Flying Reptiles

Some pterosaurs were tiny, such as the sparrow-sized Pterodactyl. Others were huge. Pterandon had wings as long as two table tennis tables. The strange horn on its head was used to balance the weight of its beak.

Furry Flier

Rhamphorhynchus was a pterosaur about the size of an eagle. It probably had a hairy body. It soared over the sea, looking for fish to eat and using its tail as a rudder.

Giant Insect

The largest insect that has ever lived was a giant dragonfly, Meganeura. Each of its wings was as long as your arm. Its main enemy was prehistoric spiders.

Webbed Feet

Hesperornis was one of the first true birds. It lived 80 million years ago, at about the same time as the first penguins. About as tall as a man, it could not fly but had powerful webbed feet for swimming.

Did You Know?

The giant bird, Aepyornis, laid eggs as big as water melons — the largest eggs ever known. Each egg would take four hours to hard boil.

The largest flying bird was a huge prehistoric vulture, Argentavis. Its wings were twice as long as those of the wandering albatross, the bird with the largest wing span alive today.

A relation of Archaeopteryx is still alive today. The hoatzin lives in South America. Like its ancestor, it has claws on its wings to help it climb up tree trunks.

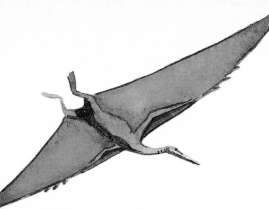

Prehistoric Plane

The largest animal ever to fly was a huge reptile called Quetzalcoaltus. It lived 65 million years ago in North America. This creature was the size of a small plane.

"Ancient Feathers"

Archaeopteryx was the first known animal to have feathers. It lived about 150 million years ago in the forests of Europe and was the size of a pigeon. Its name means "ancient feather".

Archaeopteryx's skeleton is like that of a very small dinosaur. This could mean that the birds alive now are descended from dinosaurs.

Although Archaeopteryx had feathers and a wish bone like a bird, it was also like a reptile. It had claws on its wings, jaws with sharp teeth and a tail like a lizard.

Flight Facts

The tallest bird ever could not fly. Dinornis maximus looked like an ostrich. It grew to be 11 ft (3.5 m) tall, taller than an elephant.

The largest sea bird ever lived 30 million years ago. Its wings were 19 ft (6 m) across. Today's cormorants and pelicans are descended from this giant.

The first flamingoes and owls shared the Earth with the dinosaurs, 70 million years ago. The first ducks appeared about 30 million years ago.

The earliest known bats lived 50 million years ago. Some bat fossils are so well preserved that you can even see the bat's last meal of insects inside its stomach.

Eggs and Babies

Mammals first lived on the Earth about 220 million years ago. They are different from reptiles because they are warm-blooded. Mammals have their own central heating system which keeps them warm even in very cold weather.

Today's mammals include the blue whale, the largest animal ever to have lived on Earth. The first mammals were tiny and ate insects. When the dinosaurs died out about 65 million years ago, the many different types of mammals took over the Earth.

The Changing Reptiles

About 300 million years ago, some reptiles became like mammals. These were ancestors of the first true mammals. One of first mammals, Megazostrodon, lived in Africa 190 million years ago and looked like a long-nosed mouse.

Back to the Sea

The ancestors of dolphins and whales once lived on land. They went back to live in the sea about 65 million years ago.

The biggest mammal in the sea then, a giant whale called Basilosaurus, was about 56 ft (17 m) long.

Prehistoric Pouches

Mammals with pouches, like kangaroos, where their new-born babies live and grow are called marsupials. The first marsupials lived 100 million years ago and included marsupial lions, bears and saber-toothed cats.

Horse History

The first horse, Hyracotherium, was the size of a small dog. It lived 55 million years ago in the forests of North America. Instead of hooves it had four toes on its front feet and three on its back feet.

As the Earth's weather changed over millions of years, many forests died and huge grassy plains grew in their place. Horses gradually developed hooves so they could run faster over the grass. Equus, the type of horse we see today, first lived about 2 million years ago.

Prehistoric kangaroos were twice as big as kangaroos today. Procoptodon was over 9 ft (3 m) tall. It browsed among the tree tops.

Diprotodon, the largest marsupial ever, lived in Australia about 40 million years ago. It was a huge wombat the size of a rhino.

Egg Layers

Most mammals now give birth to live babies. The first mammals probably laid eggs, like reptiles. Today there are only two mammals which lay eggs. They both live in Australia and are the duck-billed platypus and the spiny anteater, or echidna.

Did You Know?

Megatherium was the largest sloth that has ever lived. It was ten times bigger than today's sloths and was as tall as an elephant. It was too heavy to climb trees so it stood on its hind legs to pull down leaves and branches to eat.

The biggest land mammal ever was Paraceratherium. This huge rhino roamed Asia and Europe about 35 million years ago. As long as three cars, it weighed twice as much as an elephant.

The oldest known ape, Aegyptopithecus, lived in Egypt 27 million years ago. At that time Egypt was covered with hot, tropical forests.

Animal Ancestors

Over millions of years, many of the animals which lived on the Earth died out. Others changed their shape and size until they became quite different from the ones we know today.

Horns, Tusks and Headgear

Brontotherium, the "thunder beast", lived 35 million years ago. It had a massive forked horn, like a giant catapult, on its nose. It used the horn to dig up food.

Saber-toothed Stabber

The saber-toothed cat, Smilodon, was one of the fiercest mammals. It could open its huge jaws wide enough to hold a whole pig. Its dagger-like teeth were 20 times longer than human teeth.

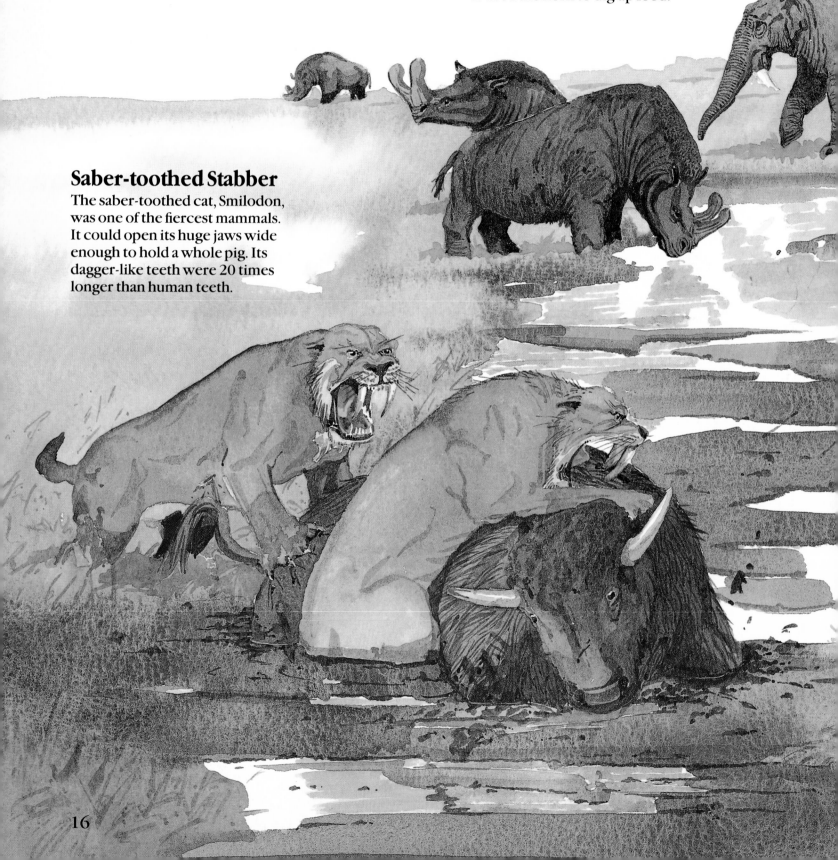

The first elephants were the size of goats and had no tusks or trunks. Later, elephants grew much bigger than they are now. Deinotherium had huge tusks curving backwards. It used them to rake the ground for roots and plants to eat.

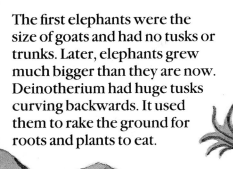

Megaloceros was the biggest deer that ever lived. Its huge antlers measured 10 ft (3 m) from tip to tip and weighed about 112 lbs (50 kg).

Did You Know?

The first meat-eating mammals appeared about 35 million years ago. The largest was Megistotherium. It was bigger than a polar bear and killed huge elephants for food.

The biggest collection of mammal fossils was found in tar pits near Los Angeles, USA. Scientists have found fossils of 40,000 animals, including 2,000 wolves, mammoths, sloths and horses, and 1,000 saber-toothed cats.

The prehistoric rhino, Elasmotherium, had a horn 12 ft (3.5 m) long. The horn grew out of a huge dome of bone on its forehead.

No Humps

Prehistoric camels had no humps. They first lived about 10 million years ago. Aepycamelus had a long neck for reaching leaves high up in the trees. Stenomylus was only the size of a deer.

Armadillo Armor

About 20 million years ago giant armadillos the size of cars lived in South America. Doedicurus had a huge, bony shell on its back and a bony club on its tail for scaring enemies. One fossil shell found had been used by early people as a tent.

Mammal Facts

Many prehistoric mammals were much larger than their modern relations and some were much smaller. Elephants living on islands in the Mediterranean were only 2.5 ft (80 cm) tall. Their cousins in Europe were six times bigger.

The first mammals probably came out at night to feed, out of sight of the dinosaurs.

The largest prehistoric rodent (the family which includes rats and mice) was Telicomys. It was the size of a small rhino.

Most mammals today are placental mammals. This means they give birth to live babies which are small versions of their parents. The first placental mammals included the ancestors of apes, monkeys and human beings.

A Long, Icy Winter

The Earth became much colder about 18,000 years ago. The ice caps at the North and South Poles grew much bigger, spreading over Scandinavia, most of Europe and the United States as far south as New York.

This Ice Age lasted for 8,000 years. One third of the world was covered with a sheet of ice which was 1.87 miles (3 km) thick in places. Some of this ancient ice still covers Greenland and the Antarctic.

Woolly Coats

As the world grew colder, some animals moved south to warmer places. Others stayed and adapted to the cold. Mammoths and rhinos grew long, woolly coats to keep them warm. Their broad feet acted like snowshoes on the ice.

Mammoth Finds

Parts of Siberia, in the USSR, are still covered by the old ice. In the last 300 years, over 5,000 mammoths have been found, deep-frozen in the ground. Rewards are still paid to local people who find them.

Mammoth Facts

In 1977 a deep-frozen baby mammoth was discovered by gold miners in the USSR. It was only 6 months old when it died 40,000 years ago.

In 1900, a frozen mammoth was found with 32 lbs (14 kg) of food in its stomach. Its last meal was grass, moss and pine needles. From them, scientists can work out what the Earth looked like when the mammoth was alive.

The largest mammoths lived in Europe about 1 million years ago. They were as tall as giraffes and as heavy as tanks.

The Indian elephant is the mammoth's closest living relative.

Woolly mammoths had huge curved tusks. The longest found are 16 ft (5 m) along the outside curve.

Cave Bears

During the last Ice Age, cave bears hibernated in the winter in large groups. The bones of over 30,000 bears were found in a cave in Austria. They may have frozen to death in their sleep.

Changing Weather

Ice Ages happen when there is a tiny change in the path the Earth takes around the Sun. Even the smallest difference can plunge the Earth into thousands of years of freezing winters.

As the ice sheets grew, the level of the seas fell by up to 330 ft (100 m). Large areas of the sea dried up. The Bering Strait between Siberia and Alaska became dry land, making a bridge 625 miles (1,000 km) wide between the USSR and North America.

We live in an Ice Age which began 3 million years ago. Each Ice Age has 17 cold periods (glacials) and 17 warm periods (interglacials). We live in an interglacial which began 10,000 years ago. The next glacial may be only 5,000 years away.

Did You Know?

For many years, people in Siberia, USSR, thought that the mammoth bones they found in the ice belonged to giant moles living deep under the ground.

In 1901, some scientists in Leningrad, USSR, ate soup made from Siberian mammoth bones. The bones were 39,000 years old.

About 450 million years ago, the Sahara was covered in thick ice and glaciers. During the last Ice Age, reindeer, woolly rhino and polar bears roamed where London, England, now stands.

The First People

Man-like creatures have been on the Earth for about 14 million years. The first true human beings, with ape-like faces, first appeared only about 2 million years ago. Modern man, who lived in Africa about 40,000 years ago, is the ancestor of everyone alive today.

Scientists have found the fossilized bones of these early peoples but we still do not know what they really looked like. But we do know where and how some of them lived, what they ate and how they made their tools and weapons.

Ape People

About 5 million until 1½ million years ago, three different types of ape-people lived in South and East Africa. They probably moved about in small groups to look for food.

They had long arms and ape-like faces with big, strong teeth and no chins. They had small brains, could not talk but only grunt, and wore no clothes.

They did not know how to make fire and ate meat raw. They also ate plants, roots, fruit, berries, birds' eggs, and other things, such as grubs.

Handy People

These people were the first true human beings and lived from about 2 million to 1½ million years ago in East Africa. They were called "handy" because they made the first known tools. They chipped at stones until they had a sharp edge.

They had bigger brains and were more intelligent. They hunted animals, cutting up the meat with stone knives. But they ate it raw as they had no fire.

Upright People

Between about 1½ million and ¼ million years ago, people began to walk upright instead of stooping like apes. They still looked a little like apes but had bigger brains and perhaps could say a few words.

They knew how to use fire and to cook meat. With fire they could frighten off animals, and they had warmth and light. They moved in search of food, staying for a few days at a camp or in a cave.

These people lived at first in Africa but gradually spread out. By about 350,000 years ago, they had reached parts of Europe and Asia.

Intelligent People

At the end of the last Ice Age, about 50,000 years ago, Neanderthal People lived in Europe. They were short, strong and were probably the first people to make clothes of animal skins to keep warm.

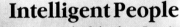

They made tools and weapons with sharp stones. They were the first people to bury their dead, putting flowers on the graves.

Neanderthal people were replaced by Cro-Magnon people, who could talk and looked very much like us.

Early People Facts

In 1912 a jaw bone was found in Britain. Scientists thought it was about a million years old and called it Piltdown Man. It turned out to be a fake, made of an orang-utan skull with teeth glued on.

Our brains are about three times bigger than our ancestors who lived 3 million years ago. Neanderthal Man had an even bigger brain but no one knows if he was more intelligent.

No one had ever said anything until about 30,000 years ago. Cro-Magnon people were the first to have throats the right shape for speaking. Before that, people made noises, pulled faces and used sign language.

No people lived in North America until about 30,000 years ago. Then people crossed from Asia over the Bering Strait which was dry land but is now under the sea.

The first people to live in Australia went there at least 30,000 years ago. The Aborigines sailed across 40 miles (60 km) of open sea from Indonesia and spread out all over the country.

Hunting for Food

Woolly mammoths, cave bears and reindeer were all hunted by the people who lived at the end of the last Ice Age. That was about 50,000 years ago when the weather was very cold.

The whole family helped to collect fruit, nuts and berries from the forests. They also dug up roots, searched for eggs, grubs and shellfish and caught fish in the rivers and lakes.

Mammoth Hunt

Hunting a mammoth was very dangerous. When the men found one, they drove it into a corner against rocks or a cliff. Then they attacked it with spears made of yew wood. The spears were hardened in a fire or had a sharp flint at the end.

Bone Huts

In the cold, flat lands of eastern Europe, there were few trees to build huts of wood, and no caves to live in. The people there hunted woolly mammoths and built huts with their bones. They put up frames of bones and tusks and covered them with mammoth skins.

Tools and Weapons

Early people made knives and axes from stones. Using one stone as a hammer, they flaked pieces off very hard stones, called flints, until they had a sharp edge.

They used stone knives to cut the skins off animals they killed. They dried the skins and sewed them into clothes. They also cut up the meat for cooking.

Bows and arrows were first used about 15,000 years ago. They were the first shooting weapons ever made. Hunters could now kill birds and small running animals.

Nothing from a mammoth was wasted. The skins were made into pants and jackets, the bones into weapons, and the meat roasted for food. It was so cold, the people stored meat in holes they dug in the ground. One mammoth could feed a family for a whole year.

Did You Know?

Scientists can work out what early people ate by looking at the scratches and worn edges on fossil teeth. One type of ape-man, nicknamed Nutcracker Man, had molar teeth four times bigger than ours. He used them to chew tough plants and crack open the shells of nuts.

Garbage dumps tell us a lot about what early people ate. The bones of about 20,000 mammoths were found in Czechoslovakia. They were the remains of meals eaten by cave people who lived about 25,000 years ago.

A garbage dump in China shows that some early people may have eaten each other. Scientists found human skulls and bones which had been smashed open to get out the brains and marrow.

23

How People Lived

For thousands of years, early people had no proper houses. They traveled from place to place, hunting the herds of animals which moved in search of fresh grass and bushes to eat.

When they found a cave, the people stayed in it for a while and then moved on again. For most of the year, they lived in tents, which were easy to put up and light enough to carry with them.

Did You Know?

The oldest houses ever found were near Nice in France. Scientists discovered the remains of oval huts which were about 450,000 years old. They were probably used for a few days a year by hunters.

There were once so many reindeer in Europe that they were Cro-Magnon people's main food. Each person may have eaten as many as a hundred reindeer every year.

Before people learned to cook meat, they starved to death if their teeth rotted and they could not chew raw meat. The first signs of toothache were found in a skull 200,000 years old.

Striking a Light

The first fires were probably started by lightning striking a dry tree. Early people learned to make fire for themselves by spinning a stick of hard, dry wood on a soft log until it smoldered. They blew on it until dry grass and leaves burst into flames. But it could take a very long time.

Later, people found they could start a fire more quickly by striking a flint on lumps of iron pyrite rock. This made sparks which set light to dry grass, leaves or bark.

The First Cooks

Meat was probably first roasted by accident when a raw lump fell on the fire. It would have smelled good and was much easier to chew and swallow than raw meat.

Early people had no pots and pans. They laid meat on mammoth bones or branches and grilled it over a fire. They also roasted meat on spits of wood or bone.

Sometimes they cooked chunks of meat in a big pit, filled with hot ashes. They boiled meat in a hollow log by dropping hot stones into the water. The cook added a few wild vegetables and roots to make a tasty stew.

When there was plenty of fish, the people gutted them and hung them over a fire to dry. They also dried strips of meat in the smoke. They ate this preserved food when other food was scarce and when traveling.

Burning Black Stones

Over 20,000 years ago, mammoth hunters in Czechoslovakia found that if they put black stones on a fire, it burned brighter and hotter. Without knowing it, they had lit the first coal fires.

Artists and Craftsmen

Prehistoric people had no metal to make tools, no cotton or wool for clothes, and no way of writing anything down. Everything they used was made of the wood and stones they found and from animals they killed.

With only wood, stones and bones, these people made fine needles, jewelery and clothes. They were the world's first painters and sculptors, leaving behind many clues to where and how they lived.

First Artists

Early artists made paints from charcoal, clay and lime. They ground them into powder and mixed them with fish glue, animal fat or blood. Seashells were used as paint pots. Animal fur, moss and frayed twigs made good brushes.

Mammoth Carving

The oldest known animal carving was found in Germany. It is a tiny horse, only 2 ins (5 cm) long, carved out of a mammoth tusk.

Early Art Galleries

The best early art gallery was found in the Lascaux caves in France. The walls are covered with 596 animals, drawn during the last Ice Age. The animals include mammoths, bison and four huge white bulls.

The caves were first found in 1940 by four boys and their dog. The dog went down a hole in the ground. When the boys went after it, they found a huge cave. Next day they took ropes and lights and saw the paintings.

Paintings, 30,000 years old, have also been found on the walls of deep caves in Spain, Africa and Australia.

No one knows why people painted these pictures. It may have been to gain magic power over the animals to make them easier to kill. The only pictures of people are stick men.

Did You Know?

The first flute players lived over 20,000 years ago. They had flutes made of reindeer antlers and bear bones. Pipes and whistles were made of hollow bird bones and doe toe bones. They were used to play music and to send messages.

The first map was drawn about 15,000 years ago by mammoth hunters in the USSR. It is carved on a mammoth tusk and shows the hunters' huts, and the trees and river near the camp.

Oldest Clothes

The oldest known clothes were found on a 37,000 year old body frozen in Siberian ground. The man was wearing animal skins, sewn together with leather strips. Early people made sewing needles from splinters of reindeer antlers.

Beads and Bracelets

People made necklaces from wolf, fox and bear teeth, snail shells and pebbles strung on strips of leather. Slices of mammoth tusk were made into bracelets. The oldest jewelery is a 35,000 year old necklace found in Czechoslovakia.

Finger Painting

Many cave walls were covered with stencils of hands, some 35,000 years old. Some hands have fingers missing. They may have been damaged by frost bite or when hunting. The stencils may be the signatures of the world's first artists.

The First Farmers

People lived by hunting animals and eating what food they could find for about three million years. Then, about 10,000 years ago, there was a great change. In the Middle East, people began to grow food and tame wild animals for milk and meat.

These people were the first farmers. Because they no longer had to search for food, they could stay in one place and build houses. The world's first town was probably Jericho in Jordan.

The First Bread

Wild wheat and barley grew in the Middle East. People collected the large seeds in their hands or cut the stalks with sickles made of wood with flint blades.

The seeds were ground between two stones into coarse brown flour. This was mixed with water and the dough was baked on hot stones to make flat, hard loaves.

Taming the Animals

The first shepherds started work about 10,000 years ago. The sheep provided meat, milk, skins and wool. They could graze on land too steep and dry to grow crops.

The first horses to be tamed were small and mainly used for pulling carts and war chariots. By about 3,500 years ago, horses had been bred which were big enough for people to ride.

Washing Up

Washing the dishes was a new task for the farmers who first made clay pots about 7,000 years ago. Before then, the early people carried water in bags made of animal skins or tree bark.

Building Bricks

As people settled down, they began to build houses with brick walls and roofs thatched with straw. The oldest known bricks were found at Jericho and are 8,000 years old. They were made of mud and straw, baked hard in the sun.

Did You Know?

Beer was first made about 8,000 years ago in the Near East.

Early farmers used deer horns to dig the ground. Ploughs were invented about 6,000 years ago.

Potatoes were grown for food in Argentina about 4,000 years ago. People first ate them in Europe only 300 years ago.

The first dogs were descended from wolves. People kept them as pets and for hunting at least 12,000 years ago.

No one knows when cats first became pets. In Ancient Egypt they were sacred to a goddess and were not kept to catch mice. This was done by a house snake.

The ancestors of cows were huge wild oxen, called aurochs. They were about 6 ft (2 m) tall and very strong. Some early farmers worshipped aurochs. An 8,000 year old shrine decorated with auroch horns was found in Turkey.

Did You Know?

The Biggest Bones

The biggest dinosaur skeleton ever found is of Brachiosaurus, in East Berlin. This dinosaur was 75 ft (23 m) long, 46 ft (14 m) tall, and weighed about 80 tons. But it may not be the largest of all. Recently two new dinosaurs have been discovered. Supersaurus and Ultrasaurus may both have weighed over 100 tons.

Biggest Bird

The biggest prehistoric bird and the biggest bird ever was Dromornis stirtoni. This giant was like an emu and lived in Australia about 11 million years ago. Fossils of its leg bones show that it was 10 ft (3 m) tall. It could not fly but was a fast runner.

Fast and Slow

Fossil footprints give scientists a good idea of how fast the dinosaurs moved. Large, lumbering creatures, such as Diplodocus, walked at about the same speed as people. One of the fastest dinosaurs, Gallimimus, could run as fast as a galloping horse.

Most Brainless

Stegosaurus was one of the most brainless creatures ever. It weighed about 2 tons but its brain was only the size of a walnut. Stegosaurus had a strange lump near its tail which people thought was a second brain. It was really a bunch of nerves which controlled the dinosaur's huge back legs and tail.

Biggest Mammal

The biggest land mammal was Paraceratherium which lived 35 million years ago. It weighed as much as four African elephants and was as tall as a giraffe. It was long enough to drive two cars, side by side, under its body.

First Flowers

The first plants grew on land about 400 million years ago but there were no flowers until about 100 million years ago. The first flowers were magnolias and water lilies, very like those which grow now. The earliest type of tree which still survives is the ginkgo tree. It first grew in China about 65 million years ago.

The Smallest

The smallest dinosaur was Compsognathus, whose name means "pretty jaw". It was only the size of a turkey, about 30 ins (75 cm) long from nose to tail and weighed just 17 lbs (7 kg).

The Longest

Diplodocus is the longest dinosaur known. At 85 ft (26 m), it was as long as a line of nine cars. From footprints found in Morocco, scientists think Breviparopus may have been longer, growing up to 158 ft (48 m). Another giant, Mamenchisaurus, had the longest neck. It was 36 ft (11 m) long—half the length of the dinosaur.

Long Neck

The huge sea reptile, Tanystropheus, had a neck longer than its body. Its neck bones were so long that scientists at first thought they must be leg bones.

Sea Giant

Kronosaurus, was the largest reptile to live in the sea. Its body was 50 ft (15 m) long and its skull was 10 ft (3 m) long with 80 terrifying teeth.

Time Ladder

The Earth's history is divided up into different periods. On the chart "mya" means "millions of years ago".

Pre-Cambrian 4,600–570 mya

Earth formed 4,600 mya
First living things 3,200 mya
First animal fossils 670 mya

Cambrian 570–500 mya

First fish 500 mya

Ordovician 500–435 mya

Many trilobites and other animals without backbones

Silurian 435–395 mya

First land plants 400 mya

Devonian 395–345 mya

First insects 380 mya
First amphibians 350 mya

Carboniferous 345–280 mya

Early reptiles 300 mya
Coal forests 300 mya

Permian 280–230 mya

More reptiles 280 mya

Triassic 230–195 mya

Early mammals 230 mya
Sea reptiles 210 mya
Flying reptiles 200 mya
First dinosaurs 200 mya

Jurassic 195–141 mya

Early mammals 190 mya
Archaeopteryx 150 mya

Cretaceous 141–65 mya

First birds 140 mya

Palaeocene 65–55 mya

Dinosaurs die out 65 mya
Mammals take over

Eocene 55–38 mya

First horses 65 mya
First elephants 40 mya

Oligocene 38–22 mya

First apes

Miocene 22–6 mya

First seals, deer, giraffes 20 mya

Pliocene 6–2 mya

Man-apes 5 mya

Pleistocene 2 mya to 10,000 years ago

First human beings 2 mya
Ice Age begins 18,000 years ago

Holocene 10,000 years ago until now

Last Ice Age ends 10,000 years ago
First farmers 10,000 years ago

Earth's History

Most of the names of the periods come from the places or the people where the rocks were first studied.

Cambrian
This period gets its name from Cambria, the Roman name for Wales.

Ordovician
Named after the Ordovices, a Celtic tribe who lived in Wales.

Silurian
Takes its name from the Silures, a Celtic tribe, which lived in the Welsh borders in Roman Britain.

Devonian
The name comes from Devonshire, a county in the southwest of Britain.

Carboniferous
When most of the coal was formed. "Carbo" is the Latin for "coal".

Permian
Named after the Perm province in the Ural Mountains, USSR.

Triassic
From three rock layers in Germany. "Treis" is the Greek for "three".

Jurassic
Called after the Jura Mountains in Switzerland and France.

Cretaceous
Named after chalk laid down in North America, Australia and Europe. "Creta" means "chalk" in Latin.

Palaoecene
The next five periods are called the Tertiary, and are also known as the "age of the mammals".

Pleistocene
The last two eras, called Quaternary, are when the remains of human beings and the things they made are found.

Index

First published in the United States of America
in 1991 by The Mallard Press
ISBN 0-7924-5522-3

Mallard Press and its accompanying design and logo are
trademarks of BDD Promotional Book Company, Inc.

Produced by Mandarin Offset
Printed and bound in Hong Kong

Edited and designed by Mitchell Beazley International Ltd.
Artists' House, 14–15 Manette Street, London W1V 5LB.

© Mitchell Beazley Publishers 1991
All rights reserved

Typeset in Garamond ITC Book by Tradespools Ltd, Frome.
Reproduction by Mandarin Offset, Hong Kong.